This manifesting checkbook belongs to

....

DREAM BELIEVE RECEIVE

MANIFESTING MY DREAMS
ASK AND YOU SHALL RECEIVE

DATE

MANIFEST TO THE
ORDER OF _____ $ [   ]

_____ DOLLARS

U LAW OF ATTRACTION

Manifestation
Universal Bank of Mind
P.O BOX 555
IN MY MIND, I WILL 333 - 000

PURPOSE _____ FROM

: 555333111 : 0000 - 55544-33333

DREAM BELIEVE RECEIVE

MANIFESTING MY DREAMS
ASK AND YOU SHALL RECEIVE

DATE

MANIFEST TO THE
ORDER OF _____ $ [   ]

_____ DOLLARS

U LAW OF ATTRACTION

Manifestation
Universal Bank of Mind
P.O BOX 555
IN MY MIND, I WILL 333 - 000

PURPOSE _____ FROM

: 555333111 : 0000 - 55544-33333

ENDORSEMENT - SIGNATURE OR STAMP

BACK/VERSO

MANIFESTED ON _____   FOR MANIFESTATION ONLY, ACCOUNT #55555-0003333

ENDORSEMENT - SIGNATURE OR STAMP

BACK/VERSO

MANIFESTED ON _____   FOR MANIFESTATION ONLY, ACCOUNT #55555-0003333

**I DREAM
I BELIEVE
I RECEIVE**

MANIFESTING MY DREAMS
ASK AND YOU SHALL RECEIVE

DATE _____

MANIFEST TO THE
ORDER OF _____ $ [_____]

_____ DOLLARS

U LAW OF
ATTRACTION

Manifestation
Universal Bank of Mind P.O BOX 555
IN MY MIND, I WILL 333 - 000

PURPOSE _____ _____ FROM

: 555333111 : 0000 - 55544-33333

**DREAM
BELIEVE
RECEIVE**

MANIFESTING MY DREAMS
ASK AND YOU SHALL RECEIVE

DATE _____

MANIFEST TO THE
ORDER OF _____ $ [_____]

_____ DOLLARS

U LAW OF
ATTRACTION

Manifestation
Universal Bank of Mind P.O BOX 555
IN MY MIND, I WILL 333 - 000

PURPOSE _____ _____ FROM

: 555333111 : 0000 - 55544-33333

ENDORSEMENT - SIGNATURE OR STAMP

BACK/VERSO

MANIFESTED ON _____   FOR MANIFESTATION ONLY, ACCOUNT #55555-00033330

ENDORSEMENT - SIGNATURE OR STAMP

BACK/VERSO

MANIFESTED ON _____   FOR MANIFESTATION ONLY, ACCOUNT #55555-00033330

MANIFESTING MY DREAMS
ASK AND YOU SHALL RECEIVE

DATE

MANIFEST TO THE
ORDER OF

$

DOLLARS

U LAW OF
ATTRACTION

Manifestation PO BOX 555
Universal Bank of Mind IN MY MIND, I WILL 333 - 000

PURPOSE

FROM

: 555333111 : 0000 - 55544-33333

MANIFESTING MY DREAMS
ASK AND YOU SHALL RECEIVE

DATE

MANIFEST TO THE
ORDER OF

$

DOLLARS

U LAW OF
ATTRACTION

Manifestation PO BOX 555
Universal Bank of Mind IN MY MIND, I WILL 333 - 000

PURPOSE

FROM

: 555333111 : 0000 - 55544-33333

DREAM
BELIEVE
RECEIVE

DREAM
BELIEVE
RECEIVE

ENDORSEMENT - SIGNATURE OR STAMP

BACK/VERSO

MANIFESTED ON _____   FOR MANIFESTATION ONLY, ACCOUNT #55555-00033330

ENDORSEMENT - SIGNATURE OR STAMP

BACK/VERSO

MANIFESTED ON _____   FOR MANIFESTATION ONLY, ACCOUNT #55555-00033330

**I DREAM
I BELIEVE
I RECEIVE**

MANIFESTING MY DREAMS
ASK AND YOU SHALL RECEIVE

DATE _____

MANIFEST TO THE
ORDER OF _____ $ [_____]

_____ DOLLARS

**◡ LAW OF
ATTRACTION**

◖ Manifestation P.O BOX 555
Universal Bank of Mind IN MY MIND, I WILL 333 - 000

PURPOSE _____ _____ FROM

: 555333111 : 0000 - 55544-33333

**DREAM
BELIEVE
RECEIVE**

MANIFESTING MY DREAMS
ASK AND YOU SHALL RECEIVE

DATE _____

MANIFEST TO THE
ORDER OF _____ $ [_____]

_____ DOLLARS

**◡ LAW OF
ATTRACTION**

◖ Manifestation P.O BOX 555
Universal Bank of Mind IN MY MIND, I WILL 333 - 000

PURPOSE _____ _____ FROM

: 555333111 : 0000 - 55544-33333

ENDORSEMENT - SIGNATURE OR STAMP

BACK/VERSO

MANIFESTED ON _____   FOR MANIFESTATION ONLY, ACCOUNT #55555-00033330

ENDORSEMENT - SIGNATURE OR STAMP

BACK/VERSO

MANIFESTED ON _____   FOR MANIFESTATION ONLY, ACCOUNT #55555-00033330

DREAM BELIEVE RECEIVE

MANIFESTING MY DREAMS
ASK AND YOU SHALL RECEIVE

DATE _____

MANIFEST TO THE
ORDER OF _____ $ [_____]

_____ DOLLARS

☋ LAW OF
ATTRACTION

◖ **Manifestation**   P.O BOX 555
Universal Bank of Mind   IN MY MIND, I WILL 333 - 000

PURPOSE _____   _____ FROM

: 555333111 : 0000 - 55544-33333

DREAM BELIEVE RECEIVE

MANIFESTING MY DREAMS
ASK AND YOU SHALL RECEIVE

DATE _____

MANIFEST TO THE
ORDER OF _____ $ [_____]

DOLLARS

☋ LAW OF
ATTRACTION

◖ **Manifestation**   P.O BOX 555
Universal Bank of Mind   IN MY MIND, I WILL 333 - 000

PURPOSE _____   _____ FROM

: 555333111 : 0000 - 55544-33333

ENDORSEMENT - SIGNATURE OR STAMP

BACK/VERSO

MANIFESTED ON _____

FOR MANIFESTATION ONLY, ACCOUNT #55555-00033330

ENDORSEMENT - SIGNATURE OR STAMP

BACK/VERSO

MANIFESTED ON _____

FOR MANIFESTATION ONLY, ACCOUNT #55555-00033330

I DREAM I BELIEVE I RECEIVE

MANIFESTING MY DREAMS
ASK AND YOU SHALL RECEIVE

DATE

MANIFEST TO THE
ORDER OF

$

DOLLARS

Manifestation
Universal Bank of Mind
PO BOX 555
IN MY MIND, I WILL 333 - 000

U LAW OF
ATTRACTION

PURPOSE

FROM

: 555333111 : 0000 - 55544-33333

DREAM BELIEVE RECEIVE

MANIFESTING MY DREAMS
ASK AND YOU SHALL RECEIVE

DATE

MANIFEST TO THE
ORDER OF

$

DOLLARS

Manifestation
Universal Bank of Mind
PO BOX 555
IN MY MIND, I WILL 333 - 000

U LAW OF
ATTRACTION

PURPOSE

FROM

: 555333111 : 0000 - 55544-33333

ENDORSEMENT - SIGNATURE OR STAMP

BACK/VERSO

MANIFESTED ON _____   FOR MANIFESTATION ONLY, ACCOUNT #55555-00033330

ENDORSEMENT - SIGNATURE OR STAMP

BACK/VERSO

MANIFESTED ON _____   FOR MANIFESTATION ONLY, ACCOUNT #55555-00033330

DREAM
BELIEVE
RECEIVE

MANIFESTING MY DREAMS
ASK AND YOU SHALL RECEIVE

DATE

MANIFEST TO THE
ORDER OF

$

DOLLARS

U LAW OF
ATTRACTION

Manifestation P.O BOX 555
Universal Bank of Mind IN MY MIND, I WILL 333 - 000

PURPOSE

FROM

: 555333111 : 0000 - 55544-33333

DREAM
BELIEVE
RECEIVE

MANIFESTING MY DREAMS
ASK AND YOU SHALL RECEIVE

DATE

MANIFEST TO THE
ORDER OF

$

DOLLARS

U LAW OF
ATTRACTION

Manifestation P.O BOX 555
Universal Bank of Mind IN MY MIND, I WILL 333 - 000

PURPOSE

FROM

: 555333111 : 0000 - 55544-33333

ENDORSEMENT - SIGNATURE OR STAMP

BACK/VERSO

MANIFESTED ON _____

FOR MANIFESTATION ONLY, ACCOUNT #55555-00033330

ENDORSEMENT - SIGNATURE OR STAMP

BACK/VERSO

MANIFESTED ON _____

FOR MANIFESTATION ONLY, ACCOUNT #55555-00033330

**I DREAM
I BELIEVE
I RECEIVE**

MANIFESTING MY DREAMS
ASK AND YOU SHALL RECEIVE

DATE _____

MANIFEST TO THE
ORDER OF _____ $ [_____]

DOLLARS

U LAW OF
ATTRACTION

◖ Manifestation P.O BOX 555
Universal Bank of Mind IN MY MIND, I WILL 333 - 000

PURPOSE _____ _____ FROM

: 555333111 : 0000 - 55544-33333

**DREAM
BELIEVE
RECEIVE**

MANIFESTING MY DREAMS
ASK AND YOU SHALL RECEIVE

DATE _____

MANIFEST TO THE
ORDER OF _____ $ [_____]

DOLLARS

U LAW OF
ATTRACTION

◖ Manifestation P.O BOX 555
Universal Bank of Mind IN MY MIND, I WILL 333 - 000

PURPOSE _____ _____ FROM

: 555333111 : 0000 - 55544-33333

ENDORSEMENT - SIGNATURE OR STAMP

BACK/VERSO

MANIFESTED ON _____

FOR MANIFESTATION ONLY, ACCOUNT #55555-00033330

ENDORSEMENT - SIGNATURE OR STAMP

BACK/VERSO

MANIFESTED ON _____

FOR MANIFESTATION ONLY, ACCOUNT #55555-00033330

DREAM BELIEVE RECEIVE

MANIFESTING MY DREAMS
ASK AND YOU SHALL RECEIVE

DATE

MANIFEST TO THE
ORDER OF

$

DOLLARS

U LAW OF
ATTRACTION

Manifestation P.O BOX 555
Universal Bank of Mind IN MY MIND, I WILL 333 - 000

PURPOSE

FROM

: 555333111 : 0000 - 55544-33333

DREAM BELIEVE RECEIVE

MANIFESTING MY DREAMS
ASK AND YOU SHALL RECEIVE

DATE

MANIFEST TO THE
ORDER OF

$

DOLLARS

U LAW OF
ATTRACTION

Manifestation P.O BOX 555
Universal Bank of Mind IN MY MIND, I WILL 333 - 000

PURPOSE

FROM

: 555333111 : 0000 - 55544-33333

ENDORSEMENT - SIGNATURE OR STAMP

BACK/VERSO

MANIFESTED ON _____

FOR MANIFESTATION ONLY, ACCOUNT #55555-00033330

ENDORSEMENT - SIGNATURE OR STAMP

BACK/VERSO

MANIFESTED ON _____

FOR MANIFESTATION ONLY, ACCOUNT #55555-00033330

I DREAM
I BELIEVE
I RECEIVE

MANIFESTING MY DREAMS
ASK AND YOU SHALL RECEIVE

DATE

MANIFEST TO THE
ORDER OF

$

DOLLARS

↻ LAW OF
ATTRACTION

Manifestation
Universal Bank of Mind

P.O BOX 555
IN MY MIND, I WILL 333 - 000

PURPOSE

FROM

: 555333111 : 0000 - 55544-33333

DREAM
BELIEVE
RECEIVE

MANIFESTING MY DREAMS
ASK AND YOU SHALL RECEIVE

DATE

MANIFEST TO THE
ORDER OF

$

DOLLARS

↻ LAW OF
ATTRACTION

Manifestation
Universal Bank of Mind

P.O BOX 555
IN MY MIND, I WILL 333 - 000

PURPOSE

FROM

: 555333111 : 0000 - 55544-33333

ENDORSEMENT - SIGNATURE OR STAMP

BACK/VERSO

MANIFESTED ON _____   FOR MANIFESTATION ONLY, ACCOUNT #55555-00033330

ENDORSEMENT - SIGNATURE OR STAMP

BACK/VERSO

MANIFESTED ON _____   FOR MANIFESTATION ONLY, ACCOUNT #55555-00033330

DREAM BELIEVE RECEIVE

MANIFESTING MY DREAMS
ASK AND YOU SHALL RECEIVE

DATE

MANIFEST TO THE
ORDER OF

$

DOLLARS

U LAW OF
ATTRACTION

Manifestation P.O BOX 555
Universal Bank of Mind IN MY MIND, I WILL 333 - 000

PURPOSE

FROM

: 555333111 : 0000 - 55544-33333

DREAM BELIEVE RECEIVE

MANIFESTING MY DREAMS
ASK AND YOU SHALL RECEIVE

DATE

MANIFEST TO THE
ORDER OF

$

DOLLARS

U LAW OF
ATTRACTION

Manifestation P.O BOX 555
Universal Bank of Mind IN MY MIND, I WILL 333 - 000

PURPOSE

FROM

: 555333111 : 0000 - 55544-33333

ENDORSEMENT - SIGNATURE OR STAMP

BACK/VERSO

MANIFESTED ON _____

FOR MANIFESTATION ONLY, ACCOUNT #55555-00033330

ENDORSEMENT - SIGNATURE OR STAMP

BACK/VERSO

MANIFESTED ON _____

FOR MANIFESTATION ONLY, ACCOUNT #55555-00033330

**I DREAM
I BELIEVE
I RECEIVE**

MANIFESTING MY DREAMS
ASK AND YOU SHALL RECEIVE

DATE

MANIFEST TO THE
ORDER OF $

DOLLARS

Manifestation
Universal Bank of Mind   P.O BOX 555
IN MY MIND, I WILL 333 - 000

⊍ LAW OF
ATTRACTION

PURPOSE   FROM

: 555333111 : 0000 - 55544-33333

**DREAM
BELIEVE
RECEIVE**

MANIFESTING MY DREAMS
ASK AND YOU SHALL RECEIVE

DATE

MANIFEST TO THE
ORDER OF $

DOLLARS

Manifestation
Universal Bank of Mind   P.O BOX 555
IN MY MIND, I WILL 333 - 000

⊍ LAW OF
ATTRACTION

PURPOSE   FROM

: 555333111 : 0000 - 55544-33333

ENDORSEMENT - SIGNATURE OR STAMP

BACK/VERSO

MANIFESTED ON _____

FOR MANIFESTATION ONLY, ACCOUNT #55555-00033330

ENDORSEMENT - SIGNATURE OR STAMP

BACK/VERSO

MANIFESTED ON _____

FOR MANIFESTATION ONLY, ACCOUNT #55555-00033330

**DREAM
BELIEVE
RECEIVE**

MANIFESTING MY DREAMS
ASK AND YOU SHALL RECEIVE

DATE

MANIFEST TO THE
ORDER OF

$

DOLLARS

U LAW OF
ATTRACTION

Manifestation
Universal Bank of Mind
P.O BOX 555
IN MY MIND, I WILL 333 - 000

PURPOSE

FROM

: 555333111 : 0000 - 55544-33333

**DREAM
BELIEVE
RECEIVE**

MANIFESTING MY DREAMS
ASK AND YOU SHALL RECEIVE

DATE

MANIFEST TO THE
ORDER OF

$

DOLLARS

U LAW OF
ATTRACTION

Manifestation
Universal Bank of Mind
P.O BOX 555
IN MY MIND, I WILL 333 - 000

PURPOSE

FROM

: 555333111 : 0000 - 55544-33333

ENDORSEMENT - SIGNATURE OR STAMP

BACK/VERSO

MANIFESTED ON _____   FOR MANIFESTATION ONLY, ACCOUNT #55555-00033330

ENDORSEMENT - SIGNATURE OR STAMP

BACK/VERSO

MANIFESTED ON _____   FOR MANIFESTATION ONLY, ACCOUNT #55555-00033330

I DREAM
I BELIEVE
I RECEIVE

MANIFESTING MY DREAMS
ASK AND YOU SHALL RECEIVE

DATE

MANIFEST TO THE
ORDER OF

$

DOLLARS

U LAW OF
ATTRACTION

Manifestation P.O BOX 555
Universal Bank of Mind IN MY MIND, I WILL 333 - 000

PURPOSE

FROM

: 555333111 : 0000 - 55544-33333

DREAM
BELIEVE
RECEIVE

MANIFESTING MY DREAMS
ASK AND YOU SHALL RECEIVE

DATE

MANIFEST TO THE
ORDER OF

$

DOLLARS

U LAW OF
ATTRACTION

Manifestation P.O BOX 555
Universal Bank of Mind IN MY MIND, I WILL 333 - 000

PURPOSE

FROM

: 555333111 : 0000 - 55544-33333

ENDORSEMENT - SIGNATURE OR STAMP

BACK/VERSO

MANIFESTED ON _____   FOR MANIFESTATION ONLY, ACCOUNT #55555-00033330

ENDORSEMENT - SIGNATURE OR STAMP

BACK/VERSO

MANIFESTED ON _____   FOR MANIFESTATION ONLY, ACCOUNT #55555-00033330

MANIFESTING MY DREAMS
ASK AND YOU SHALL RECEIVE

DATE

MANIFEST TO THE
ORDER OF $

                                                              DOLLARS
                                                              U LAW OF
                                                              ATTRACTION

Manifestation P.O BOX 555
Universal Bank of Mind IN MY MIND, I WILL 333 - 000

PURPOSE   FROM

: 555333111 : 0000 - 55544-33333

DREAM
BELIEVE
RECEIVE

MANIFESTING MY DREAMS
ASK AND YOU SHALL RECEIVE

DATE

MANIFEST TO THE
ORDER OF $

                                                              DOLLARS
                                                              U LAW OF
                                                              ATTRACTION

Manifestation P.O BOX 555
Universal Bank of Mind IN MY MIND, I WILL 333 - 000

PURPOSE   FROM

: 555333111 : 0000 - 55544-33333

ENDORSEMENT - SIGNATURE OR STAMP

BACK/VERSO

MANIFESTED ON _____

FOR MANIFESTATION ONLY, ACCOUNT #55555-00033330

ENDORSEMENT - SIGNATURE OR STAMP

BACK/VERSO

MANIFESTED ON _____

FOR MANIFESTATION ONLY, ACCOUNT #55555-00033330

MANIFESTING MY DREAMS

ASK AND YOU SHALL RECEIVE

DATE _____

MANIFEST TO THE
ORDER OF _____ $ [   ]

_____ DOLLARS

U LAW OF
ATTRACTION

Manifestation P.O BOX 555
Universal Bank of Mind IN MY MIND, I WILL 333 - 000

PURPOSE _____ FROM _____

: 555333111 : 0000 - 55544-33333

MANIFESTING MY DREAMS

ASK AND YOU SHALL RECEIVE

DATE _____

MANIFEST TO THE
ORDER OF _____ $ [   ]

_____ DOLLARS

U LAW OF
ATTRACTION

Manifestation P.O BOX 555
Universal Bank of Mind IN MY MIND, I WILL 333 - 000

PURPOSE _____ FROM _____

: 555333111 : 0000 - 55544-33333

ENDORSEMENT - SIGNATURE OR STAMP

BACK/VERSO

MANIFESTED ON _____

FOR MANIFESTATION ONLY, ACCOUNT #55555-00033330

ENDORSEMENT - SIGNATURE OR STAMP

BACK/VERSO

MANIFESTED ON _____

FOR MANIFESTATION ONLY, ACCOUNT #55555-00033330

DREAM
BELIEVE
RECEIVE

MANIFESTING MY DREAMS
ASK AND YOU SHALL RECEIVE

DATE

MANIFEST TO THE
ORDER OF _____ $ [   ]

DOLLARS

U LAW OF
ATTRACTION

◨ Manifestation P.O BOX 555
Universal Bank of Mind IN MY MIND, I WILL 333 - 000

PURPOSE _____ FROM

: 555333111 : 0000 - 55544-33333

DREAM
BELIEVE
RECEIVE

MANIFESTING MY DREAMS
ASK AND YOU SHALL RECEIVE

DATE

MANIFEST TO THE
ORDER OF _____ $ [   ]

DOLLARS

U LAW OF
ATTRACTION

◨ Manifestation P.O BOX 555
Universal Bank of Mind IN MY MIND, I WILL 333 - 000

PURPOSE _____ FROM

: 555333111 : 0000 - 55544-33333

ENDORSEMENT - SIGNATURE OR STAMP

BACK/VERSO

MANIFESTED ON _____   FOR MANIFESTATION ONLY, ACCOUNT #55555-00033330

ENDORSEMENT - SIGNATURE OR STAMP

BACK/VERSO

MANIFESTED ON _____   FOR MANIFESTATION ONLY, ACCOUNT #55555-00033330

**I DREAM
I BELIEVE
I RECEIVE**

MANIFESTING MY DREAMS
ASK AND YOU SHALL RECEIVE

DATE

MANIFEST TO THE
ORDER OF

$

DOLLARS

U LAW OF
ATTRACTION

Manifestation
Universal Bank of Mind

P.O BOX 555
IN MY MIND, I WILL 333 - 000

PURPOSE

FROM

: 555333111 : 0000 - 55544-33333

**DREAM
BELIEVE
RECEIVE**

MANIFESTING MY DREAMS
ASK AND YOU SHALL RECEIVE

DATE

MANIFEST TO THE
ORDER OF

$

DOLLARS

U LAW OF
ATTRACTION

Manifestation
Universal Bank of Mind

P.O BOX 555
IN MY MIND, I WILL 333 - 000

PURPOSE

FROM

: 555333111 : 0000 - 55544-33333

ENDORSEMENT - SIGNATURE OR STAMP

BACK/VERSO

MANIFESTED ON _____   FOR MANIFESTATION ONLY, ACCOUNT #55555-00033330

ENDORSEMENT - SIGNATURE OR STAMP

BACK/VERSO

MANIFESTED ON _____   FOR MANIFESTATION ONLY, ACCOUNT #55555-00033330

MANIFESTING MY DREAMS
ASK AND YOU SHALL RECEIVE

DATE _____

MANIFEST TO THE
ORDER OF _____ $ [_____]

_____ DOLLARS

U LAW OF
ATTRACTION

Manifestation P.O BOX 555
Universal Bank of Mind IN MY MIND, I WILL 333 - 000

PURPOSE _____ FROM

⑈ 555333111 ⑈ 0000 - 55544-33333

DREAM BELIEVE RECEIVE

MANIFESTING MY DREAMS
ASK AND YOU SHALL RECEIVE

DATE _____

MANIFEST TO THE
ORDER OF _____ $ [_____]

_____ DOLLARS

U LAW OF
ATTRACTION

Manifestation P.O BOX 555
Universal Bank of Mind IN MY MIND, I WILL 333 - 000

PURPOSE _____ FROM

⑈ 555333111 ⑈ 0000 - 55544-33333

ENDORSEMENT - SIGNATURE OR STAMP

BACK/VERSO

MANIFESTED ON _____   FOR MANIFESTATION ONLY, ACCOUNT #55555-00033330

ENDORSEMENT - SIGNATURE OR STAMP

BACK/VERSO

MANIFESTED ON _____   FOR MANIFESTATION ONLY, ACCOUNT #55555-00033330

**I DREAM
I BELIEVE
I RECEIVE**

MANIFESTING MY DREAMS
ASK AND YOU SHALL RECEIVE

DATE

MANIFEST TO THE
ORDER OF

$

DOLLARS

☡ LAW OF
ATTRACTION

Manifestation
Universal Bank of Mind
P.O BOX 555
IN MY MIND, I WILL 333 - 000

PURPOSE

FROM

: 555333111 : 0000 - 55544-33333

**DREAM
BELIEVE
RECEIVE**

MANIFESTING MY DREAMS
ASK AND YOU SHALL RECEIVE

DATE

MANIFEST TO THE
ORDER OF

$

DOLLARS

☡ LAW OF
ATTRACTION

Manifestation
Universal Bank of Mind
P.O BOX 555
IN MY MIND, I WILL 333 - 000

PURPOSE

FROM

: 555333111 : 0000 - 55544-33333

ENDORSEMENT - SIGNATURE OR STAMP

BACK/VERSO

MANIFESTED ON _____

FOR MANIFESTATION ONLY, ACCOUNT #55555-00033330

ENDORSEMENT - SIGNATURE OR STAMP

BACK/VERSO

MANIFESTED ON _____

FOR MANIFESTATION ONLY, ACCOUNT #55555-00033330

DREAM BELIEVE RECEIVE

MANIFESTING MY DREAMS
ASK AND YOU SHALL RECEIVE

DATE

MANIFEST TO THE
ORDER OF

$

DOLLARS

U LAW OF
ATTRACTION

Manifestation
Universal Bank of Mind
P.O BOX 555
IN MY MIND, I WILL 333 - 000

PURPOSE

FROM

: 555333111 : 0000 - 55544-33333

DREAM BELIEVE RECEIVE

MANIFESTING MY DREAMS
ASK AND YOU SHALL RECEIVE

DATE

MANIFEST TO THE
ORDER OF

$

DOLLARS

U LAW OF
ATTRACTION

Manifestation
Universal Bank of Mind
P.O BOX 555
IN MY MIND, I WILL 333 - 000

PURPOSE

FROM

: 555333111 : 0000 - 55544-33333

ENDORSEMENT - SIGNATURE OR STAMP

BACK/VERSO

MANIFESTED ON _____   FOR MANIFESTATION ONLY, ACCOUNT #55555-00033330

ENDORSEMENT - SIGNATURE OR STAMP

BACK/VERSO

MANIFESTED ON _____   FOR MANIFESTATION ONLY, ACCOUNT #55555-00033330

I DREAM
I BELIEVE
I RECEIVE

MANIFESTING MY DREAMS
ASK AND YOU SHALL RECEIVE

DATE ____________

MANIFEST TO THE ORDER OF ____________ $ [ ]

____________ DOLLARS

LAW OF ATTRACTION

Manifestation
Universal Bank of Mind
P.O BOX 555
IN MY MIND, I WILL 333 - 000

PURPOSE ____________ FROM ____________

: 555333111 : 0000 - 55544-33333

DREAM
BELIEVE
RECEIVE

MANIFESTING MY DREAMS
ASK AND YOU SHALL RECEIVE

DATE ____________

MANIFEST TO THE ORDER OF ____________ $ [ ]

____________ DOLLARS

LAW OF ATTRACTION

Manifestation
Universal Bank of Mind
P.O BOX 555
IN MY MIND, I WILL 333 - 000

PURPOSE ____________ FROM ____________

: 555333111 : 0000 - 55544-33333

ENDORSEMENT - SIGNATURE OR STAMP

BACK/VERSO

MANIFESTED ON _____

FOR MANIFESTATION ONLY, ACCOUNT #55555-00033330

ENDORSEMENT - SIGNATURE OR STAMP

BACK/VERSO

MANIFESTED ON _____

FOR MANIFESTATION ONLY, ACCOUNT #55555-00033330

**DREAM
BELIEVE
RECEIVE**

MANIFESTING MY DREAMS
ASK AND YOU SHALL RECEIVE

DATE

MANIFEST TO THE
ORDER OF _____ $ [   ]

_____ DOLLARS

**☡ LAW OF
ATTRACTION**

◩ **Manifestation** P.O BOX 555
Universal Bank of Mind IN MY MIND, I WILL · 333 - 000

PURPOSE _____ FROM

: 555333111 : 0000 - 55544-33333

**DREAM
BELIEVE
RECEIVE**

MANIFESTING MY DREAMS
ASK AND YOU SHALL RECEIVE

DATE

MANIFEST TO THE
ORDER OF _____ $ [   ]

_____ DOLLARS

**☡ LAW OF
ATTRACTION**

◩ **Manifestation** P.O BOX 555
Universal Bank of Mind IN MY MIND, I WILL 333 - 000

PURPOSE _____ FROM

: 555333111 : 0000 - 55544-33333

ENDORSEMENT - SIGNATURE OR STAMP

BACK/VERSO

MANIFESTED ON _____   FOR MANIFESTATION ONLY, ACCOUNT #55555-00033330

ENDORSEMENT - SIGNATURE OR STAMP

BACK/VERSO

MANIFESTED ON _____   FOR MANIFESTATION ONLY, ACCOUNT #55555-00033330

**I DREAM
I BELIEVE
I RECEIVE**

MANIFESTING MY DREAMS
ASK AND YOU SHALL RECEIVE

DATE

MANIFEST TO THE
ORDER OF _____ $ [_____]

DOLLARS
U LAW OF
ATTRACTION

Manifestation
Universal Bank of Mind
P.O BOX 555
IN MY MIND, I WILL 333 - 000

PURPOSE _____ FROM

: 555333111 : 0000 - 55544-33333

**DREAM
BELIEVE
RECEIVE**

MANIFESTING MY DREAMS
ASK AND YOU SHALL RECEIVE

DATE

MANIFEST TO THE
ORDER OF _____ $ [_____]

DOLLARS
U LAW OF
ATTRACTION

Manifestation
Universal Bank of Mind
P.O BOX 555
IN MY MIND, I WILL 333 - 000

PURPOSE _____ FROM

: 555333111 : 0000 - 55544-33333

ENDORSEMENT - SIGNATURE OR STAMP

BACK/VERSO

MANIFESTED ON _____   FOR MANIFESTATION ONLY, ACCOUNT #55555-00033330

ENDORSEMENT - SIGNATURE OR STAMP

BACK/VERSO

MANIFESTED ON _____   FOR MANIFESTATION ONLY, ACCOUNT #55555-00033330

DREAM
BELIEVE
RECEIVE

MANIFESTING MY DREAMS
ASK AND YOU SHALL RECEIVE

DATE

MANIFEST TO THE
ORDER OF

$

DOLLARS

U LAW OF
ATTRACTION

Manifestation P.O BOX 555
Universal Bank of Mind IN MY MIND, I WILL 333 - 000

PURPOSE

FROM

: 555333111 : 0000 - 55544-33333

DREAM
BELIEVE
RECEIVE

MANIFESTING MY DREAMS
ASK AND YOU SHALL RECEIVE

DATE

MANIFEST TO THE
ORDER OF

$

DOLLARS

U LAW OF
ATTRACTION

Manifestation P.O BOX 555
Universal Bank of Mind IN MY MIND, I WILL 333 - 000

PURPOSE

FROM

: 555333111 : 0000 - 55544-33333

ENDORSEMENT - SIGNATURE OR STAMP

BACK/VERSO

MANIFESTED ON _____

FOR MANIFESTATION ONLY, ACCOUNT #55555-00033330

ENDORSEMENT - SIGNATURE OR STAMP

BACK/VERSO

MANIFESTED ON _____

FOR MANIFESTATION ONLY, ACCOUNT #55555-00033330

**I DREAM
I BELIEVE
I RECEIVE**

MANIFESTING MY DREAMS
ASK AND YOU SHALL RECEIVE

DATE _____

MANIFEST TO THE
ORDER OF _____ $ [_____]

DOLLARS
U LAW OF
ATTRACTION

Manifestation
Universal Bank of Mind   P.O. BOX 555
IN MY MIND, I WILL 333 - 000

PURPOSE _____   FROM _____

: 555333111 : 0000 - 55544-33333

**DREAM
BELIEVE
RECEIVE**

MANIFESTING MY DREAMS
ASK AND YOU SHALL RECEIVE

DATE _____

MANIFEST TO THE
ORDER OF _____ $ [_____]

DOLLARS
U LAW OF
ATTRACTION

Manifestation
Universal Bank of Mind   P.O. BOX 555
IN MY MIND, I WILL 333 - 000

PURPOSE _____   FROM _____

: 555333111 : 0000 - 55544-33333

ENDORSEMENT - SIGNATURE OR STAMP

BACK/VERSO

MANIFESTED ON _____   FOR MANIFESTATION ONLY, ACCOUNT #55555-00033330

ENDORSEMENT - SIGNATURE OR STAMP

BACK/VERSO

MANIFESTED ON _____   FOR MANIFESTATION ONLY, ACCOUNT #55555-00033330

DREAM BELIEVE RECEIVE

MANIFESTING MY DREAMS
ASK AND YOU SHALL RECEIVE

DATE _____

MANIFEST TO THE
ORDER OF _____ $ [_____]

_____ DOLLARS

U LAW OF
ATTRACTION

Manifestation
Universal Bank of Mind P.O BOX 555
IN MY MIND, I WILL 333 - 000

PURPOSE _____ _____ FROM

: 555333111 : 0000 - 55544-33333

DREAM BELIEVE RECEIVE

MANIFESTING MY DREAMS
ASK AND YOU SHALL RECEIVE

DATE _____

MANIFEST TO THE
ORDER OF _____ $ [_____]

_____ DOLLARS

U LAW OF
ATTRACTION

Manifestation
Universal Bank of Mind P.O BOX 555
IN MY MIND, I WILL 333 - 000

PURPOSE _____ _____ FROM

: 555333111 : 0000 - 55544-33333

ENDORSEMENT - SIGNATURE OR STAMP

BACK/VERSO

MANIFESTED ON _____

FOR MANIFESTATION ONLY, ACCOUNT #55555-00033330

ENDORSEMENT - SIGNATURE OR STAMP

BACK/VERSO

MANIFESTED ON _____

FOR MANIFESTATION ONLY, ACCOUNT #55555-00033330

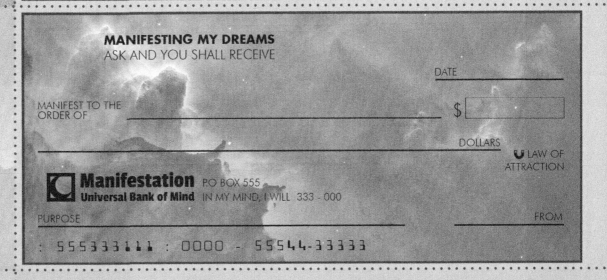

**I DREAM
I BELIEVE
I RECEIVE**

MANIFESTING MY DREAMS
ASK AND YOU SHALL RECEIVE

DATE _____

MANIFEST TO THE
ORDER OF _____ $ [_____]

_____ DOLLARS

☩ LAW OF
ATTRACTION

◖ Manifestation P.O BOX 555
Universal Bank of Mind IN MY MIND, I WILL 333 - 000

PURPOSE _____ FROM _____

: 555333111 : 0000 - 55544-33333

**DREAM
BELIEVE
RECEIVE**

MANIFESTING MY DREAMS
ASK AND YOU SHALL RECEIVE

DATE _____

MANIFEST TO THE
ORDER OF _____ $ [_____]

_____ DOLLARS

☩ LAW OF
ATTRACTION

◖ Manifestation P.O BOX 555
Universal Bank of Mind IN MY MIND, I WILL 333 - 000

PURPOSE _____ FROM _____

: 555333111 : 0000 - 55544-33333

ENDORSEMENT - SIGNATURE OR STAMP

BACK/VERSO

MANIFESTED ON _____   FOR MANIFESTATION ONLY, ACCOUNT #55555-00033330

ENDORSEMENT - SIGNATURE OR STAMP

BACK/VERSO

MANIFESTED ON _____   FOR MANIFESTATION ONLY, ACCOUNT #55555-00033330

DREAM
BELIEVE
RECEIVE

MANIFESTING MY DREAMS
ASK AND YOU SHALL RECEIVE

DATE

MANIFEST TO THE
ORDER OF

$

DOLLARS

U LAW OF
ATTRACTION

Manifestation
Universal Bank of Mind   P.O BOX 555
IN MY MIND, I WILL 333 - 000

PURPOSE

FROM

: 555333111 : 0000 - 55544-33333

DREAM
BELIEVE
RECEIVE

MANIFESTING MY DREAMS
ASK AND YOU SHALL RECEIVE

DATE

MANIFEST TO THE
ORDER OF

$

DOLLARS

U LAW OF
ATTRACTION

Manifestation
Universal Bank of Mind   P.O BOX 555
IN MY MIND, I WILL 333 - 000

PURPOSE

FROM

: 555333111 : 0000 - 55544-33333

ENDORSEMENT - SIGNATURE OR STAMP

BACK/VERSO

MANIFESTED ON _____

FOR MANIFESTATION ONLY, ACCOUNT #55555-00033330

ENDORSEMENT - SIGNATURE OR STAMP

BACK/VERSO

MANIFESTED ON _____

FOR MANIFESTATION ONLY, ACCOUNT #55555-00033330

**I DREAM
I BELIEVE
I RECEIVE**

MANIFESTING MY DREAMS
ASK AND YOU SHALL RECEIVE

DATE

MANIFEST TO THE
ORDER OF _____ $ [   ]

DOLLARS

U LAW OF
ATTRACTION

Manifestation
Universal Bank of Mind   P.O BOX 555
IN MY MIND, I WILL 333 - 000

PURPOSE _____ FROM

: 555333111 : 0000 - 55544-33333

**DREAM
BELIEVE
RECEIVE**

MANIFESTING MY DREAMS
ASK AND YOU SHALL RECEIVE

DATE

MANIFEST TO THE
ORDER OF _____ $ [   ]

DOLLARS

U LAW OF
ATTRACTION

Manifestation
Universal Bank of Mind   P.O BOX 555
IN MY MIND, I WILL 333 - 000

PURPOSE _____ FROM

: 555333111 : 0000 - 55544-33333

ENDORSEMENT - SIGNATURE OR STAMP

BACK/VERSO

MANIFESTED ON _____

FOR MANIFESTATION ONLY, ACCOUNT #55555-00033330

ENDORSEMENT - SIGNATURE OR STAMP

BACK/VERSO

MANIFESTED ON _____

FOR MANIFESTATION ONLY, ACCOUNT #55555-00033330

**DREAM
BELIEVE
RECEIVE**

MANIFESTING MY DREAMS
ASK AND YOU SHALL RECEIVE

DATE

MANIFEST TO THE
ORDER OF

$

DOLLARS

U LAW OF
ATTRACTION

Manifestation
Universal Bank of Mind
P.O BOX 555
IN MY MIND, I WILL 333 - 000

PURPOSE

FROM

: 555333111 : 0000 - 55544-33333

**DREAM
BELIEVE
RECEIVE**

MANIFESTING MY DREAMS
ASK AND YOU SHALL RECEIVE

DATE

MANIFEST TO THE
ORDER OF

$

DOLLARS

U LAW OF
ATTRACTION

Manifestation
Universal Bank of Mind
P.O BOX 555
IN MY MIND, I WILL 333 - 000

PURPOSE

FROM

: 555333111 : 0000 - 55544-33333

ENDORSEMENT - SIGNATURE OR STAMP

BACK/VERSO

MANIFESTED ON _____ FOR MANIFESTATION ONLY, ACCOUNT #55555-00033330

ENDORSEMENT - SIGNATURE OR STAMP

BACK/VERSO

MANIFESTED ON _____ FOR MANIFESTATION ONLY, ACCOUNT #55555-00033330

**I DREAM
I BELIEVE
I RECEIVE**

MANIFESTING MY DREAMS
ASK AND YOU SHALL RECEIVE

DATE

MANIFEST TO THE
ORDER OF _____

$ _____

_____

DOLLARS

☋ LAW OF
ATTRACTION

▢ Manifestation P.O BOX 555
Universal Bank of Mind IN MY MIND, I WILL 333 - 000

PURPOSE _____

FROM

: 555333111 : 0000 - 55544-33333

**DREAM
BELIEVE
RECEIVE**

MANIFESTING MY DREAMS
ASK AND YOU SHALL RECEIVE

DATE

MANIFEST TO THE
ORDER OF _____

$ _____

_____

DOLLARS

☋ LAW OF
ATTRACTION

▢ Manifestation P.O BOX 555
Universal Bank of Mind IN MY MIND, I WILL 333 - 000

PURPOSE _____

FROM

: 555333111 : 0000 - 55544-33333

ENDORSEMENT - SIGNATURE OR STAMP

BACK/VERSO

MANIFESTED ON _____   FOR MANIFESTATION ONLY, ACCOUNT #55555-00033330

ENDORSEMENT - SIGNATURE OR STAMP

BACK/VERSO

MANIFESTED ON _____   FOR MANIFESTATION ONLY, ACCOUNT #55555-00033330

**DREAM
BELIEVE
RECEIVE**

MANIFESTING MY DREAMS
ASK AND YOU SHALL RECEIVE

DATE _____

MANIFEST TO THE
ORDER OF _____ $ [   ]

_____ DOLLARS

U LAW OF
ATTRACTION

Manifestation
Universal Bank of Mind   P.O BOX 555
IN MY MIND, I WILL 333 - 000

PURPOSE _____   FROM _____

: 555333111 : 0000 - 55544-33333

**DREAM
BELIEVE
RECEIVE**

MANIFESTING MY DREAMS
ASK AND YOU SHALL RECEIVE

DATE _____

MANIFEST TO THE
ORDER OF _____ $ [   ]

_____ DOLLARS

U LAW OF
ATTRACTION

Manifestation
Universal Bank of Mind   P.O BOX 555
IN MY MIND, I WILL 333 - 000

PURPOSE _____   FROM _____

: 555333111 : 0000 - 55544-33333

ENDORSEMENT - SIGNATURE OR STAMP

BACK/VERSO

MANIFESTED ON _____   FOR MANIFESTATION ONLY, ACCOUNT #55555-00033330

ENDORSEMENT - SIGNATURE OR STAMP

BACK/VERSO

MANIFESTED ON _____   FOR MANIFESTATION ONLY, ACCOUNT #55555-00033330

**I DREAM
I BELIEVE
I RECEIVE**

MANIFESTING MY DREAMS
ASK AND YOU SHALL RECEIVE

DATE

MANIFEST TO THE
ORDER OF

$

DOLLARS

☋ LAW OF
ATTRACTION

Manifestation
Universal Bank of Mind
P.O. BOX 555
IN MY MIND, I WILL 333 - 000

PURPOSE

FROM

: 555333111 : 0000 - 55544-33333

**DREAM
BELIEVE
RECEIVE**

MANIFESTING MY DREAMS
ASK AND YOU SHALL RECEIVE

DATE

MANIFEST TO THE
ORDER OF

$

DOLLARS

☋ LAW OF
ATTRACTION

Manifestation
Universal Bank of Mind
P.O. BOX 555
IN MY MIND, I WILL 333 - 000

PURPOSE

FROM

: 555333111 : 0000 - 55544-33333

ENDORSEMENT - SIGNATURE OR STAMP

BACK/VERSO

MANIFESTED ON _____

FOR MANIFESTATION ONLY, ACCOUNT #55555-00033330

ENDORSEMENT - SIGNATURE OR STAMP

BACK/VERSO

MANIFESTED ON _____

FOR MANIFESTATION ONLY, ACCOUNT #55555-00033330

DREAM
BELIEVE
RECEIVE

MANIFESTING MY DREAMS
ASK AND YOU SHALL RECEIVE

DATE

MANIFEST TO THE
ORDER OF

$

DOLLARS

U LAW OF
ATTRACTION

Manifestation P.O BOX 555
Universal Bank of Mind IN MY MIND, I WILL 333 - 000

PURPOSE

FROM

: 555333111 : 0000 - 55544-33333

DREAM
BELIEVE
RECEIVE

MANIFESTING MY DREAMS
ASK AND YOU SHALL RECEIVE

DATE

MANIFEST TO THE
ORDER OF

$

DOLLARS

U LAW OF
ATTRACTION

Manifestation P.O BOX 555
Universal Bank of Mind IN MY MIND, I WILL 333 - 000

PURPOSE

FROM

: 555333111 : 0000 - 55544-33333

ENDORSEMENT - SIGNATURE OR STAMP

BACK/VERSO

MANIFESTED ON _____

FOR MANIFESTATION ONLY, ACCOUNT #55555-00033330

ENDORSEMENT - SIGNATURE OR STAMP

BACK/VERSO

MANIFESTED ON _____

FOR MANIFESTATION ONLY, ACCOUNT #55555-00033330

**I DREAM
I BELIEVE
I RECEIVE**

MANIFESTING MY DREAMS
ASK AND YOU SHALL RECEIVE

DATE

MANIFEST TO THE
ORDER OF

$

DOLLARS

�*U* LAW OF
ATTRACTION

Manifestation
Universal Bank of Mind
P.O BOX 555
IN MY MIND, I WILL 333 - 000

PURPOSE

FROM

: 555333111 : 0000 - 55544-33333

**DREAM
BELIEVE
RECEIVE**

MANIFESTING MY DREAMS
ASK AND YOU SHALL RECEIVE

DATE

MANIFEST TO THE
ORDER OF

$

DOLLARS

�*U* LAW OF
ATTRACTION

Manifestation
Universal Bank of Mind
P.O BOX 555
IN MY MIND, I WILL 333 - 000

PURPOSE

FROM

: 555333111 : 0000 - 55544-33333

ENDORSEMENT - SIGNATURE OR STAMP

BACK/VERSO

MANIFESTED ON _____   FOR MANIFESTATION ONLY, ACCOUNT #55555-00033330

ENDORSEMENT - SIGNATURE OR STAMP

BACK/VERSO

MANIFESTED ON _____   FOR MANIFESTATION ONLY, ACCOUNT #55555-00033330

MANIFESTING MY DREAMS
ASK AND YOU SHALL RECEIVE

DATE

MANIFEST TO THE
ORDER OF

$

DOLLARS

U LAW OF
ATTRACTION

Manifestation
Universal Bank of Mind
P.O BOX 555
IN MY MIND, I WILL 333 - 000

PURPOSE

FROM

: 555333111 : 0000 - 55544-33333

MANIFESTING MY DREAMS
ASK AND YOU SHALL RECEIVE

DATE

MANIFEST TO THE
ORDER OF

$

DOLLARS

U LAW OF
ATTRACTION

Manifestation
Universal Bank of Mind
P.O BOX 555
IN MY MIND, I WILL 333 - 000

PURPOSE

FROM

: 555333111 : 0000 - 55544-33333

ENDORSEMENT - SIGNATURE OR STAMP

BACK/VERSO

MANIFESTED ON _____

FOR MANIFESTATION ONLY, ACCOUNT #55555-00033330

ENDORSEMENT - SIGNATURE OR STAMP

BACK/VERSO

MANIFESTED ON _____

FOR MANIFESTATION ONLY, ACCOUNT #55555-00033330

I DREAM
I BELIEVE
I RECEIVE

MANIFESTING MY DREAMS
ASK AND YOU SHALL RECEIVE

DATE

MANIFEST TO THE
ORDER OF

$

DOLLARS

↻ LAW OF
ATTRACTION

Manifestation
Universal Bank of Mind

P.O BOX 555
IN MY MIND, I WILL 333 - 000

PURPOSE

FROM

: 555333111 : 0000 - 55544-33333

DREAM
BELIEVE
RECEIVE

MANIFESTING MY DREAMS
ASK AND YOU SHALL RECEIVE

DATE

MANIFEST TO THE
ORDER OF

$

DOLLARS

↻ LAW OF
ATTRACTION

Manifestation
Universal Bank of Mind

P.O BOX 555
IN MY MIND, I WILL 333 - 000

PURPOSE

FROM

: 555333111 : 0000 - 55544-33333

ENDORSEMENT - SIGNATURE OR STAMP

BACK/VERSO

MANIFESTED ON _____   FOR MANIFESTATION ONLY, ACCOUNT #55555-00033330

ENDORSEMENT - SIGNATURE OR STAMP

BACK/VERSO

MANIFESTED ON _____   FOR MANIFESTATION ONLY, ACCOUNT #55555-00033330

DREAM
BELIEVE
RECEIVE

MANIFESTING MY DREAMS
ASK AND YOU SHALL RECEIVE

DATE _____

MANIFEST TO THE
ORDER OF _____ $ [_____]

_____ DOLLARS

U LAW OF
ATTRACTION

Manifestation
Universal Bank of Mind P.O BOX 555
IN MY MIND, I WILL 333 - 000

PURPOSE _____ FROM

: 555333111 : 0000 - 55544-33333

DREAM
BELIEVE
RECEIVE

MANIFESTING MY DREAMS
ASK AND YOU SHALL RECEIVE

DATE _____

MANIFEST TO THE
ORDER OF _____ $ [_____]

_____ DOLLARS

U LAW OF
ATTRACTION

Manifestation
Universal Bank of Mind P.O BOX 555
IN MY MIND, I WILL 333 - 000

PURPOSE _____ FROM

: 555333111 : 0000 - 55544-33333

ENDORSEMENT - SIGNATURE OR STAMP

BACK/VERSO

MANIFESTED ON _____

FOR MANIFESTATION ONLY, ACCOUNT #55555-00033330

ENDORSEMENT - SIGNATURE OR STAMP

BACK/VERSO

MANIFESTED ON _____

FOR MANIFESTATION ONLY, ACCOUNT #55555-00033330

I DREAM
I BELIEVE
I RECEIVE

MANIFESTING MY DREAMS
ASK AND YOU SHALL RECEIVE

DATE _____

MANIFEST TO THE
ORDER OF _____ $ [   ]

_____ DOLLARS

↻ LAW OF
ATTRACTION

Manifestation P.O BOX 555
Universal Bank of Mind IN MY MIND, I WILL 333 - 000

PURPOSE _____ FROM

: 555333111 : 0000 - 55544-33333

DREAM
BELIEVE
RECEIVE

MANIFESTING MY DREAMS
ASK AND YOU SHALL RECEIVE

DATE _____

MANIFEST TO THE
ORDER OF _____ $ [   ]

_____ DOLLARS

↻ LAW OF
ATTRACTION

Manifestation P.O BOX 555
Universal Bank of Mind IN MY MIND, I WILL 333 - 000

PURPOSE _____ FROM

: 555333111 : 0000 - 55544-33333

ENDORSEMENT - SIGNATURE OR STAMP

BACK/VERSO

MANIFESTED ON _____   FOR MANIFESTATION ONLY, ACCOUNT #55555-00033330

ENDORSEMENT - SIGNATURE OR STAMP

BACK/VERSO

MANIFESTED ON _____   FOR MANIFESTATION ONLY, ACCOUNT #55555-00033330

DREAM BELIEVE RECEIVE

MANIFESTING MY DREAMS
ASK AND YOU SHALL RECEIVE

DATE _____

MANIFEST TO THE
ORDER OF _____ $ [_____]

_____ DOLLARS

U LAW OF
ATTRACTION

Manifestation
Universal Bank of Mind   P.O BOX 555
IN MY MIND, I WILL 333 - 000

PURPOSE _____   FROM

: 555333111 : 0000 - 55544-33333

DREAM BELIEVE RECEIVE

MANIFESTING MY DREAMS
ASK AND YOU SHALL RECEIVE

DATE _____

MANIFEST TO THE
ORDER OF _____ $ [_____]

_____ DOLLARS

U LAW OF
ATTRACTION

Manifestation
Universal Bank of Mind   P.O BOX 555
IN MY MIND, I WILL 333 - 000

PURPOSE _____   FROM

: 555333111 : 0000 - 55544-33333

ENDORSEMENT - SIGNATURE OR STAMP

BACK/VERSO

MANIFESTED ON _____

FOR MANIFESTATION ONLY, ACCOUNT #55555-00033330

ENDORSEMENT - SIGNATURE OR STAMP

BACK/VERSO

MANIFESTED ON _____

FOR MANIFESTATION ONLY, ACCOUNT #55555-00033330

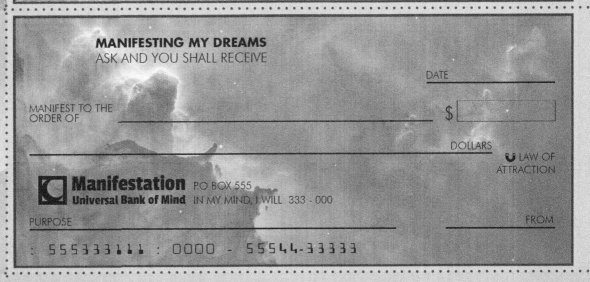

I DREAM
I BELIEVE
I RECEIVE

MANIFESTING MY DREAMS
ASK AND YOU SHALL RECEIVE

DATE _____

MANIFEST TO THE
ORDER OF _____ $ [   ]

DOLLARS

◡ LAW OF
ATTRACTION

Manifestation   P.O BOX 555
Universal Bank of Mind   IN MY MIND, I WILL   333 - 000

PURPOSE _____   _____ FROM

: 555333111 : 0000 - 55544-33333

DREAM
BELIEVE
RECEIVE

MANIFESTING MY DREAMS
ASK AND YOU SHALL RECEIVE

DATE _____

MANIFEST TO THE
ORDER OF _____ $ [   ]

DOLLARS

◡ LAW OF
ATTRACTION

Manifestation   P.O BOX 555
Universal Bank of Mind   IN MY MIND, I WILL   333 - 000

PURPOSE _____   _____ FROM

: 555333111 : 0000 - 55544-33333

ENDORSEMENT - SIGNATURE OR STAMP

BACK/VERSO

MANIFESTED ON _____

FOR MANIFESTATION ONLY, ACCOUNT #55555-00033330

ENDORSEMENT - SIGNATURE OR STAMP

BACK/VERSO

MANIFESTED ON _____

FOR MANIFESTATION ONLY, ACCOUNT #55555-00033330

DREAM BELIEVE RECEIVE

MANIFESTING MY DREAMS
ASK AND YOU SHALL RECEIVE

DATE

MANIFEST TO THE
ORDER OF

$

DOLLARS

U LAW OF
ATTRACTION

Manifestation
Universal Bank of Mind
P.O BOX 555
IN MY MIND, I WILL 333 - 000

PURPOSE

FROM

: 555333111 : 0000 - 55544-33333

DREAM BELIEVE RECEIVE

MANIFESTING MY DREAMS
ASK AND YOU SHALL RECEIVE

DATE

MANIFEST TO THE
ORDER OF

$

DOLLARS

U LAW OF
ATTRACTION

Manifestation
Universal Bank of Mind
P.O BOX 555
IN MY MIND, I WILL 333 - 000

PURPOSE

FROM

: 555333111 : 0000 - 55544-33333

ENDORSEMENT - SIGNATURE OR STAMP

BACK/VERSO

MANIFESTED ON _____

FOR MANIFESTATION ONLY, ACCOUNT #55555-00033330

ENDORSEMENT - SIGNATURE OR STAMP

BACK/VERSO

MANIFESTED ON _____

FOR MANIFESTATION ONLY, ACCOUNT #55555-00033330

**I DREAM
I BELIEVE
I RECEIVE**

MANIFESTING MY DREAMS
ASK AND YOU SHALL RECEIVE

DATE

MANIFEST TO THE
ORDER OF

$

DOLLARS

U LAW OF
ATTRACTION

Manifestation
Universal Bank of Mind

P.O BOX 555
IN MY MIND, I WILL 333 - 000

PURPOSE

FROM

: 555333111 : 0000 - 55544-33333

**DREAM
BELIEVE
RECEIVE**

MANIFESTING MY DREAMS
ASK AND YOU SHALL RECEIVE

DATE

MANIFEST TO THE
ORDER OF

$

DOLLARS

U LAW OF
ATTRACTION

Manifestation
Universal Bank of Mind

P.O BOX 555
IN MY MIND, I WILL 333 - 000

PURPOSE

FROM

: 555333111 : 0000 - 55544-33333

ENDORSEMENT - SIGNATURE OR STAMP

BACK/VERSO

MANIFESTED ON _____   FOR MANIFESTATION ONLY, ACCOUNT #55555-00033330

ENDORSEMENT - SIGNATURE OR STAMP

BACK/VERSO

MANIFESTED ON _____   FOR MANIFESTATION ONLY, ACCOUNT #55555-00033330

DREAM BELIEVE RECEIVE

MANIFESTING MY DREAMS
ASK AND YOU SHALL RECEIVE

DATE

MANIFEST TO THE ORDER OF

$

DOLLARS

U LAW OF ATTRACTION

◧ **Manifestation** P.O BOX 555
Universal Bank of Mind IN MY MIND, I WILL 333 - 000

PURPOSE

FROM

: 555333111 : 0000 - 55544-33333

DREAM BELIEVE RECEIVE

MANIFESTING MY DREAMS
ASK AND YOU SHALL RECEIVE

DATE

MANIFEST TO THE ORDER OF

$

DOLLARS

U LAW OF ATTRACTION

◧ **Manifestation** P.O BOX 555
Universal Bank of Mind IN MY MIND, I WILL 333 - 000

PURPOSE

FROM

: 555333111 : 0000 - 55544-33333

ENDORSEMENT - SIGNATURE OR STAMP

BACK/VERSO

MANIFESTED ON _____

FOR MANIFESTATION ONLY, ACCOUNT #55555-00033330

ENDORSEMENT - SIGNATURE OR STAMP

BACK/VERSO

MANIFESTED ON _____

FOR MANIFESTATION ONLY, ACCOUNT #55555-00033330

**I DREAM
I BELIEVE
I RECEIVE**

MANIFESTING MY DREAMS
ASK AND YOU SHALL RECEIVE

DATE _____

MANIFEST TO THE
ORDER OF _____ $ [_____]

DOLLARS

◡ LAW OF
ATTRACTION

◖ Manifestation P.O. BOX 555
Universal Bank of Mind IN MY MIND, I WILL 333 - 000

PURPOSE _____ _____ FROM

: 555333111 : 0000 - 55544-33333

**DREAM
BELIEVE
RECEIVE**

MANIFESTING MY DREAMS
ASK AND YOU SHALL RECEIVE

DATE _____

MANIFEST TO THE
ORDER OF _____ $ [_____]

DOLLARS

◡ LAW OF
ATTRACTION

◖ Manifestation P.O. BOX 555
Universal Bank of Mind IN MY MIND, I WILL 333 - 000

PURPOSE _____ _____ FROM

: 555333111 : 0000 - 55544-33333

ENDORSEMENT - SIGNATURE OR STAMP

BACK/VERSO

MANIFESTED ON _____   FOR MANIFESTATION ONLY, ACCOUNT #55555-00033330

ENDORSEMENT - SIGNATURE OR STAMP

BACK/VERSO

MANIFESTED ON _____   FOR MANIFESTATION ONLY, ACCOUNT #55555-00033330

MANIFESTING MY DREAMS
ASK AND YOU SHALL RECEIVE

DATE

MANIFEST TO THE
ORDER OF _____ $ [   ]

DOLLARS

Manifestation P.O BOX 555
Universal Bank of Mind IN MY MIND, I WILL 333 - 000

☋ LAW OF
ATTRACTION

PURPOSE _____ FROM _____

: 555333111 : 0000 - 55544-33333

MANIFESTING MY DREAMS
ASK AND YOU SHALL RECEIVE

DATE

MANIFEST TO THE
ORDER OF _____ $ [   ]

DOLLARS

Manifestation P.O BOX 555
Universal Bank of Mind IN MY MIND, I WILL 333 - 000

☋ LAW OF
ATTRACTION

PURPOSE _____ FROM _____

: 555333111 : 0000 - 55544-33333

ENDORSEMENT - SIGNATURE OR STAMP

BACK/VERSO

MANIFESTED ON _____   FOR MANIFESTATION ONLY, ACCOUNT #55555-00033330

ENDORSEMENT - SIGNATURE OR STAMP

BACK/VERSO

MANIFESTED ON _____   FOR MANIFESTATION ONLY, ACCOUNT #55555-00033330

**I DREAM
I BELIEVE
I RECEIVE**

MANIFESTING MY DREAMS
ASK AND YOU SHALL RECEIVE

DATE

MANIFEST TO THE
ORDER OF _____

$ [   ]

DOLLARS

_____

U LAW OF
ATTRACTION

Manifestation
Universal Bank of Mind

P.O. BOX 555
IN MY MIND, I WILL 333 - 000

PURPOSE _____

FROM _____

: 555333111 : 0000 - 55544-33333

**DREAM
BELIEVE
RECEIVE**

MANIFESTING MY DREAMS
ASK AND YOU SHALL RECEIVE

DATE

MANIFEST TO THE
ORDER OF _____

$ [   ]

DOLLARS

_____

U LAW OF
ATTRACTION

Manifestation
Universal Bank of Mind

P.O. BOX 555
IN MY MIND, I WILL 333 - 000

PURPOSE _____

FROM _____

: 555333111 : 0000 - 55544-33333

ENDORSEMENT - SIGNATURE OR STAMP

BACK/VERSO

MANIFESTED ON _____

FOR MANIFESTATION ONLY, ACCOUNT #55555-00033330

ENDORSEMENT - SIGNATURE OR STAMP

BACK/VERSO

MANIFESTED ON _____

FOR MANIFESTATION ONLY, ACCOUNT #55555-00033330

MANIFESTING MY DREAMS
ASK AND YOU SHALL RECEIVE

DATE

MANIFEST TO THE
ORDER OF

$

DOLLARS

U LAW OF
ATTRACTION

Manifestation
Universal Bank of Mind   P.O BOX 555
IN MY MIND, I WILL 333 - 000

PURPOSE

FROM

: 555333111 : 0000 - 55544-33333

MANIFESTING MY DREAMS
ASK AND YOU SHALL RECEIVE

DATE

MANIFEST TO THE
ORDER OF

$

DOLLARS

U LAW OF
ATTRACTION

Manifestation
Universal Bank of Mind   P.O BOX 555
IN MY MIND, I WILL 333 - 000

PURPOSE

FROM

: 555333111 : 0000 - 55544-33333

ENDORSEMENT - SIGNATURE OR STAMP

BACK/VERSO

MANIFESTED ON _____

FOR MANIFESTATION ONLY, ACCOUNT #55555-00033330

ENDORSEMENT - SIGNATURE OR STAMP

BACK/VERSO

MANIFESTED ON _____

FOR MANIFESTATION ONLY, ACCOUNT #55555-00033330

MANIFESTING MY DREAMS
ASK AND YOU SHALL RECEIVE

DATE _____

MANIFEST TO THE
ORDER OF _____ $ [   ]

DOLLARS _____

U LAW OF
ATTRACTION

Manifestation P.O BOX 555
Universal Bank of Mind IN MY MIND, I WILL 333 - 000

PURPOSE _____ FROM

: 555333111 : 0000 - 55544-33333

MANIFESTING MY DREAMS
ASK AND YOU SHALL RECEIVE

DATE _____

MANIFEST TO THE
ORDER OF _____ $ [   ]

DOLLARS _____

U LAW OF
ATTRACTION

Manifestation P.O BOX 555
Universal Bank of Mind IN MY MIND, I WILL 333 - 000

PURPOSE _____ FROM

: 555333111 : 0000 - 55544-33333

ENDORSEMENT - SIGNATURE OR STAMP

BACK/VERSO

MANIFESTED ON _____

FOR MANIFESTATION ONLY, ACCOUNT #55555-00033330

ENDORSEMENT - SIGNATURE OR STAMP

BACK/VERSO

MANIFESTED ON _____

FOR MANIFESTATION ONLY, ACCOUNT #55555-00033330

Made in the USA
Las Vegas, NV
23 December 2024

15288502R00057